NATIVE AMERICAN ART

Petra Press

Heinemann
LIBRARY

www.heinemann.co.uk/library
Visit our website to find out more information about Heinemann Library books.

To order:
☎ Phone 44 (0) 1865 888066
🖹 Send a fax to 44 (0) 1865 314091
💻 Visit the Heinemann Bookshop at www.heinemann.co.uk/library to browse our catalogue and order online.

First published in Great Britain by Heinemann Library, Halley Court, Jordan Hill, Oxford, OX2 8EJ, a division of Reed Educational and Professional Publishing Ltd.
Heinemann is a registered trademark of Reed Educational and Professional Publishing Ltd.

OXFORD MELBOURNE AUCKLAND
JOHANNESBURG BLANTYRE GABORONE
IBADAN PORTSMOUTH NH (USA) CHICAGO

Originated by Dot Gradations
Printed in Wing King Tong in Hong Kong.

ISBN 0 431 05590 4 (hardback)   ISBN 0 431 05595 5
05 04 03 02 01   06 05 04 03 02 01
10 9 8 7 6 5 4 3 2   10 9 8 7 6 5 4 3 2 1

British Library Cataloguing in Publication Data

Press, Petra
   Native American art - (Art in history)
   1.Indian art - North America
   I.Title
   704'.0397

Acknowledgments

© Art Resource/Werner Forman, 5; © Corbis/Morton Beebe, S.F., 6; © Corbis/Buddy Mays, 7; © Corbis/Richard Hamilton Smith, 8; © Corbis/David Muench, 9; © American Museum Natural History/Neg./Transparency No. 319175. Courtesy Department of Library Services, 10; © National Museum of American Art/Smithsonian American Art Museum, Gift of Mrs. Joseph Harrison, Jr., 11; © Corbis/Richard A Cooke, 12; © Art Resource/Werner Forman Archive, Private Collection, 13; © Brooklyn Museum/"Panther Effigy Pipe", USA, Indiana, AD 1-4000 Black steatite 6.0 x 17.t x 4.0 cm, Anonymous loan L49.5, 14; © Ohio Historical Society, 15; © Art Resource/The Newark Museum, Newark, New Jersey, 16; © Art Resource/Werner Forman Archive, Museum of Anthropology, University of British Columbia, Canada, 17; © National Museum of the American Indian, 18; © Portland Art Museum/Portland Art Museum, Portland, Oregon, Axel Rasmussen Collection, purchased with the Indian Collection Subscription Fund, 19; © Corbis/Richard A Cooke, 20; © Corbis/David Muench, 21; © National Museum of the American Indian/Courtesy, National Museum of the American Indian, Smithsonian Institution (Neg# 15/0855) Photo by David Heald, 22; © Art Resource/Werner Forman Archive, British Museum, London, 23; © Corbis/Ted Spiegel, 24; © Corbis/Buddy Mays, 25; © Photo Researchers, Inc./Georg Gerster, 26; © Saint Louis Art Musuem/Eliza McMillan Fund, 27; © Bernice Steinbaum Gallery/Jeff Sturges, 28

Cover photograph reproduced with permission of © National Museum of the American Indian.

Every effort has been made to contact copyright holders of any material reproduced in this book. Any omissions will be rectified in subsequent printings if notice is given to the publisher.

Some words are shown in bold, **like this.** You can find out what they mean by looking in the Glossary.

CONTENTS

In this book, dates are followed by the letters BCE (Before Common Era) or CE (Common Era). This is instead of using BC (Before Christ) and AD (*Anno Domini*), meaning in the year of our Lord.

WHAT IS NATIVE AMERICAN ART?

Native American cultures have existed in North America for thousands of years. Over 500 different Native American nations were spread over seven major areas, which are sometimes called **culture areas**. These areas are now called the Northwest Pacific Coast, California, Basin Plateau, Southwest, Great Plains, Southeast and Eastern Woodlands. Each of these nations has a rich culture that is thousands of years old, and has its own history, government, religion and myths.

Communities of Native North Americans developed artistic skills to express their beliefs and history in a variety of ways, just as people did in other parts of the world. The beautiful objects the Native Americans created always had a social or religious use. Creating art and practising religion were part of everyday life because even **functional** objects were designed to remind people of their beliefs, traditions and history.

This map shows the different culture areas in North America.

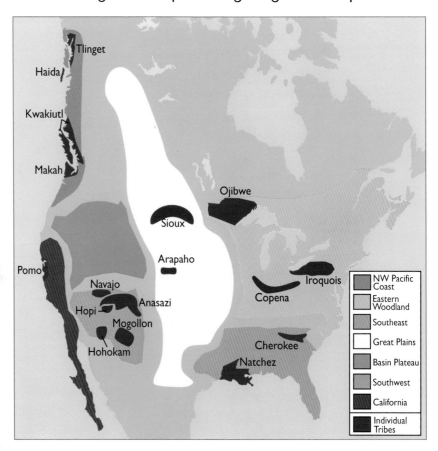

	NW Pacific Coast
	Eastern Woodland
	Southeast
	Great Plains
	Basin Plateau
	Southwest
	California
	Individual Tribes

Tlinget
Haida
Kwakiutl
Makah
Ojibwe
Sioux
Arapaho
Pomo
Navajo
Anasazi
Hopi
Mogollon
Hohokam
Copena
Iroquois
Cherokee
Natchez

Each culture developed a unique and recognizable style, although neighbouring communities often traded their skills and materials. Everyone created functional art objects, but in every area there were specialists who were more skilled than others. Whether it was carving a **ceremonial** pipe, weaving a basket or blanket, or painting a battle scene on a rock wall, each artist worked with great care so that the object would contribute to the harmony and beauty of the world.

Lakota Sioux painting on buckskin.

Works like this were often painted to show the owner's skills in battle. The paintings were also used as historical documents for people to find out about their history and heroes.

New tools and designs

Until the arrival of European settlers, Native Americans used painstaking traditional techniques to create their everyday and ceremonial art. The settlers introduced chemical dyes, the potter's wheel, metalworking and the sewing needle, making it easier for Native Americans to produce some of their art. This European influence also had a negative effect. Early settlers wanted to trade goods for Native American pottery, baskets and textiles, but thought the designs were **primitive**. Over the years, many Native American artists began to change the colour, shape and size of their creations to meet the demands of the white traders.

SIGNS AND SYMBOLS

While no two Native American cultures developed exactly the same religion, most believed that spirits lived in the animals, rocks, rivers, land and trees around them. Therefore, every being had a soul that had to be respected. When a hunter killed a deer for food, he thanked the animal for its **sacrifice** and then buried its bones so that its spirit could be reborn.

Native Americans believed that all life should be in harmony with its environment. **Shamans** held **rituals** to call on certain spirits to heal sickness and to protect the community from its enemies. Shamans carved and painted special masks, pipes, **rattles**, and **amulets** in the shapes of the spirits whose help they needed. Tlingit shamans in the Northwest Pacific Coast **culture area** asked the sea otter for help, while shamans in the Plains culture area called on the buffalo.

Totem pole, Kwakiutl people, British Columbia, cedar wood.

Totem poles were carved from one large tree trunk. Each animal spirit carved on the pole had a specific meaning and importance for the owner.

Other tribe members carved amulets that they carried for protection against enemies and sickness. Often the person also carried an amulet in the shape of his or her animal spirit. The animal spirits and natural world are important symbols in Native American art.

Teenage boys spent months preparing for a **vision quest**, a **spiritual** event that sent the teenager on a long hike away from the village with no food and water. The teenager would stay away from the village until an animal came to him in a dream. He then took the animal spirit's name, such as Running Deer or Spotted Eagle, as his own and returned to the village as an adult. Bears, deer, wolves, birds and frogs all served as animal spirits.

Kachina, Hopi people, Arizona, wood.

The Hopi believe that each kachina carving can pass on some of the power of the kachina spirit it represents.

Kachinas
Hopi dancers wore carved and painted wooden masks in a ceremony to thank spirits they called kachinas for a bountiful harvest. Small kachina dolls were intricately carved in one piece of wood or one piece of the root of a cotton plant, then brightly painted. Kachinas were given to babies as amulets to bring them good health and a long life.

ROCK ART

Paintings and carvings on rocks or cave walls, known as rock art, were used to record battles, history and other important tribal events. Some cultures used rock art to tell religious stories. Over 2500 years ago, the Anasazi Indians of the Southwest **culture area** painted **pictographs** of human figures on the sandstone rock of desert canyons, and the Great Plains people painted pictographs in the Midwest, near the Great Lakes. Painted in bright yellows and reds, the pictures showed people hunting animals or fighting each other. Many were of people playing flutes and other musical instruments. The most common paintings are red and white hand prints of children and adults, believed to have been placed there during religious ceremonies.

Pictograph, Hegman Lake, Minnesota, red paint on rock.

This pictograph shows a hunter with his prey.

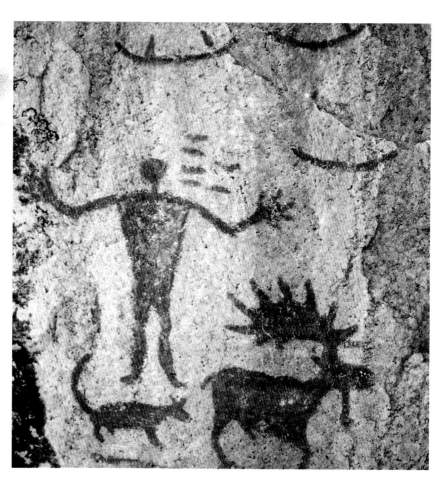

Petroglyphs

The rock art found throughout the rest of North America was created over a thousand years later. In addition to pictograph paintings of animal spirits, some cultures used a different kind of rock art, called **petroglyphs**. Petroglyphs were images, or a sort of picture alphabet, carved into rock to record a tribe's history, to serve as a symbol in important ceremonies or to show detailed maps of hunting locations. These forms of rock art are important because by examining them we can learn a lot about the way people used to live.

Petroglyph, Wind River Range, Wyoming, carving on rock.

*This figure was probably carved by a **shaman** in a ceremony to ensure a successful hunt.*

USING TREES AND PLANTS

Native Americans of the Eastern Woodlands **culture area** used the bark of white birch trees to make hundreds of useful objects. It was light, easy to work with, waterproof, did not rot in hot weather, and so was perfect for constructing canoes and covering **wigwams**. People also used it to make storage containers, hunting and fishing gear, musical instruments, decorative fans and even children's sledges and other toys. Birch bark was also used to write on, since it is durable and light enough to be carried around.

Records, Ojibwe people, birch bark, about 17th century.

*These records are easy to read, even after being handled by many people. They were made by the Ojibwe people who were part of the Midewiwin group. This was a secret society of **shamans**. It was formed to protect people from new diseases that had been brought by the white settlers. The members kept notes about their meetings on birch bark.*

Portrait of an Iroquois Wife, *George Catlin.*

This portrait (painted about 1835CE) shows a cradle made with branches and plant fibres.

Native Americans also used the roots and twigs of willow, spruce and pine trees, as well as plants such as cat-tails and corn husks to create household objects, bows and arrows, children's toys and cradles and **ceremonial** masks and **rattles**. Plant fibres could easily be bent into many different shapes. Using plant fibres gave the finished objects interesting textures and colours.

WOOD SCULPTURE

Wood carving was especially popular along the Northwest Pacific Coast **culture area** where large planks were cut from trees to construct houses big enough to hold dozens of people. People built canoes that were large enough to hunt whales out on the ocean, and carved tall poles decorated with their family's **totems** and guardian animal spirits. They also carved helmets, shields and clubs to use in battle. Almost all of their carved objects, whether large or small, were richly painted. Paint was made from bark, berries and moss. The artist painted the carving using a paintbrush made of porcupine hair.

*Carved wood **rattle**, Makah people, Washington.*

Rattles were used in religious ceremonies, or to emphasize parts of important speeches.

The potlatch
Northwest Pacific Coast peoples stored enough of the food they had hunted, fished and gathered in the summer to be able to spend the winter throwing elaborate feasts and parties called **potlatches**. It was traditional to give each guest a beautifully carved or woven gift. The more elaborate the gifts, the higher the host's status in the community. The gifts were often ornately carved serving bowls or intricately designed blankets.

Wood carving was highly developed in the densely-forested Eastern Woodlands and Northwest Pacific Coast culture areas. It was not common in the deserts of the Southwest, because fewer trees grew there. People living in and near forests used wood for just about everything, including tool handles, containers to store food and clothing, **ceremonial** masks and rattles, as well as for everyday objects such as serving bowls and spoons. These items were often carved in the shapes of beavers, hawks, snakes and other animals.

In the Southeast culture area, mask carving was a highly developed speciality. The Cherokee carved **cougar** masks for ceremonies to honour the cougar and to give the hunters cat-like hunting abilities. They also carved masks for ceremonies like the Boogerman Dance, a dance that was performed to scare away evil spirits that tried to harm their crops. They painted and decorated the wooden masks with animal fur, quills, feathers, toenails and even teeth

Mask of a beaver and killer whale, Kwakiutl people, British Columbia, about 1700CE.

Masks such as this were used in elaborate ceremonial dances. Kwakiutl masks had parts that could move for more dramatic ceremonies.

STONE SCULPTURE

Native North Americans carved stone as well as wood to make objects such as bowls, farming tools, **ceremonial** figures and arrowheads. Tools made out of harder rock were used to carve soft rock such as **limestone**, soapstone and catlinite. Limestone was used for larger statues because it is less heavy than other types of rock. Soapstone, so called because it feels like soap, was popular for smaller items, such as pipes and bowls, because it is soft and easily carved. Catlinite, also known as **pipestone**, is a special form of hard red clay that could be used for the stems and bowls of ceremonial pipes in which tobacco could be burnt. Some important pipes were called **effigy pipes**. These pipes came in all sizes and animal shapes, although cats and other graceful animals were the most popular. Some pipes were for everyday use, but most effigy pipes were used for ceremonies and **rituals**.

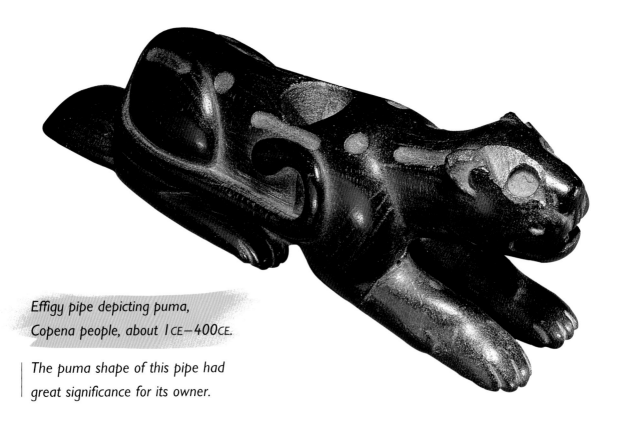

Effigy pipe depicting puma, Copena people, about 1 CE–400CE.

The puma shape of this pipe had great significance for its owner.

After the Europeans introduced metal tools to North America, some Native Americans, such as the Haida of the Northwest Pacific Coast **culture area**, started carving boxes and other objects out of harder rocks such as argulite and black shale. In addition to animal designs, such as the raven and whale, people carved their first impressions of the European traders and settlers who landed on their coasts.

Platform effigy pipe in the shape of a frog, Copena people, about 1 CE – 400 CE.

This effigy pipe is carved from catlinite, which is often called pipestone. The pipe was used during important ceremonies.

Metals
Native North American artists did not use much metal until the Europeans introduced new ways of refining iron, gold and silver in the 16th century. Copper was the only metal they used before then. Some cultures in the Northwest Pacific Coast culture area pounded copper into thin decorative plates, which were given as gifts at the elaborate **potlatch** parties held each winter.

BASKETRY

Native Americans in the Great Plains and the Southwest were weaving baskets over 11,000 years ago. The Anasazi, **ancestors** of the Pueblo people in the Southwest **culture area**, used baskets for everything from baby cradles to funeral jars. They also used baskets to gather and store food. Bowl-shaped baskets were woven so tightly that they were waterproof. These baskets were used as hats or to transport water, and could also be used to cook food.

*Pomo **ceremonial** gift basket, Pomo people, California, willow, feathers, abalone shells, about 19th century.*

During the 19th century, the Pomo people made coiled baskets like this to sell to white settlers in California. They sold the baskets to raise money to buy back their land from the settlers.

Weaving and coiling

There were two main ways of making baskets: weaving and coiling. Both methods used all kinds of grasses, roots, bark and other plant materials. Weaving – pulling softer fibres in and out of stiffer fibres that formed the basic basket shape – produced the strongest baskets. Coiling – wrapping a long, thick strand of fibre round and round, and then sewing the coils together – was a faster method, but the baskets were not as strong. Finished baskets were often decorated with animal designs or tribal symbols. Plant dyes were used to colour the materials shades of red, yellow, black, purple, green-blue, brown and white. Weavers often decorated the finished baskets with feathers, quills, shells, leather or beads. Size varied from small **trinket** baskets to storage jars that were over one-metre tall, and that could take as long as two years to make.

Basket with killer whale design, Tlingit people, Alaska, woven roots of the spruce tree

Baskets like this one were useful as well as beautiful. This basket is woven, not coiled.

TEXTILES

Fabric weaving is a lot like basket weaving, since it consists of threading strips of one material over and under stronger strips of another. However, preparing the materials for weaving cloth is more difficult and the methods took thousands of years longer to evolve. By 700CE, the Anasazi had developed a simple upright loom (a large square made of wooden poles that held the stronger fibres in place). The cloth that they wove from cactus fibre and hemp plants resembles the cotton that is woven today. It was used to make blankets, **serapes**, shawls, shoes and bags. Because **sacred** symbols and designs were woven into the fabrics, weaving was considered a sacred occupation. Women, and in some cultures, men, were therefore regarded as weavers of the thread of life.

Navajo blanket, wool,
Navajo people, Arizona.

Navajo blankets are still made
on looms made by the weaver.

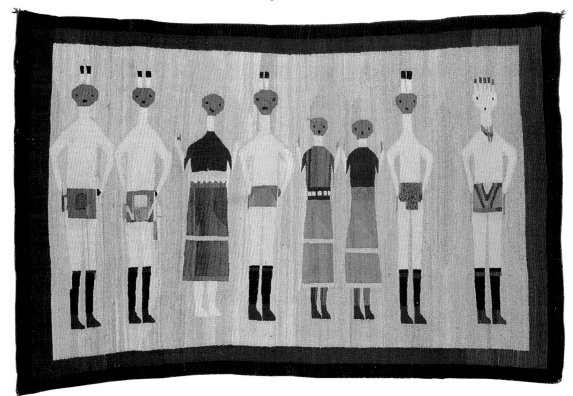

Weaving materials

In addition to plant fibres, weavers used feathers and the fur of animals such as rabbits and dogs. The weaving of wool did not begin until the Spanish introduced sheep into the Southwest **culture area** around 1600CE. Other popular sources of weaving materials that were used after the arrival of Europeans in the continent were the old uniforms, army blankets and red flannel underwear that white settlers traded to Native Americans. The Native Americans **unravelled** these and redyed the wool before weaving it into their own designs to make blankets and clothing.

Chilkat weave shirt, Tlingit people, Alaska, cedar bark and mountain goat wool weave with fur lining.

The Chilkat weave symbolized wealth. Sometimes wealthy people burned these shirts and robes as proof of their wealth and status.

POTTERY

The first **nomadic** Native Americans used lightweight baskets to gather and store food. Pottery developed much later, when people discovered that if they smeared baskets with clay and then dried them, they would hold water. By the year 200BCE, the Hohokam people of the Southwest **culture area** were moulding bowls and jars out of wet clay. Potters' wheels did not exist until Europeans introduced them in the 16th century. Instead, a potter would use the bottom of a broken pot to form the base of a new one. He or she rolled coils of clay to form the walls of the bowl or jug, pinched the coils together, shaped the pot with tools made from **gourds** or sticks, and then smoothed it with water. The pottery was hardened over an outdoor fire, often using dried animal dung for fuel.

Pottery, Anasazi people, Mesa Verde, Colorado, about 600CE–1300CE.

This pottery was found in Mesa Verde, an Anasazi city built high on the cliffs of Colorado.

Mimbres burial pottery

Pottery also played a major role in religious ceremonies and **rituals**. When **archaeologists** excavated the Mogollon people's burial sites in the Mimbres area, they discovered skeletal remains with clay bowls covering the heads. Magical images of clouds, animals and spirits were painted on the interiors of each bowl. Each bowl had a hole in the bottom so that the person's spirit could escape.

By 700CE, people in the Southwest culture area were painting their pottery in striking black and white designs. The artists chewed the ends of twigs to make their brushes. They also began making small, animal-shaped **ceremonial** figures and pipes out of clay. Over time, individual villages became known for their different pot shapes and decorative styles, which included animal and insect shapes and geometric patterns. Yellow and red became the traditional colours in some areas, while some cultures continued to use black and white.

With the exception of some parts of the Northwest Pacific Coast culture area, pottery developed all over North America, although it was never as beautifully shaped and painted as it was in the Southwest.

Pot with bat, Mogollon people, Gila Cliff Dwellings, New Mexico, about 950–1350CE.

This pot was made to be used in a burial. We can tell that it was never used because it does not have a hole in the bottom.

21

JEWELLERY AND HEADDRESSES

Many Native North Americans wore jewellery or other kinds of body decoration to show that they belonged to a certain **clan** or tribe. The jewellery was often a tooth, claw or other animal part carried as a **totem**, or it was an **amulet**, hair ornament or necklace made out of beads, shells or feathers. Items like these were often given to teenagers to celebrate their passage into adulthood after their **vision quest**, or to young men when they became warriors. Beads and feathers also decorated clothing worn to celebrate weddings or other special ceremonies. Necklaces made of shells were worn to prevent illness, while **shamans** often wore red face-paint and red hair ornaments to cure a sickness.

Disk with crested woodpeckers, shell, about 1250–1300CE.

This disc was carved to decorate a necklace. The woodpeckers carved on it would have had great importance for the owner of the necklace.

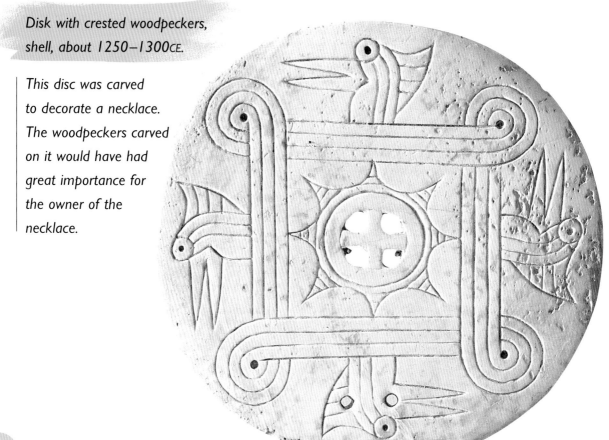

After the Europeans introduced them to North America in the 16th century, Native Americans added glass beads to their jewellery and clothing designs. In some cultures, men and women wore **wampum** beads to show they were important tribal members. The beads were also used as money to trade for other goods.

Many Native American cultures also came to be known for their featherwork. People wore feathers as jewellery, or on clothing and headdresses to show their position in society, and some feathers were worn in **spiritual** ceremonies. One common belief was that a feather represented the qualities of the bird it came from. Cherokee tribes considered owl, hummingbird, eagle, turkey and buzzard feathers to be especially powerful. They believed that owl feathers represented wisdom, while eagle feathers represented honour and success.

War bonnet, Arapaho people, eagle feathers, shells, beads and leather.

War bonnets such as this were worn by tribes that lived on the Plains. This bonnet is fairly short. Some of them had feathers that reached all the way down to the wearer's knees!

SANDPAINTINGS

According to Navajo legend, Holy People **animate** all things, including animals, people, trees, winds, rivers, even colours and the four directions. The Holy People teach about the harmony of the universe. The Navajo believe that to keep the Holy People happy, everything must be kept in balance. When a Navajo is sick or has misfortune, it is because bad spirits have entered his or her body, and he or she has thrown the balance of the universe out of harmony. To regain health or fortune, the person must ask an *Hatathli,* which means 'singer' in Navajo, to conduct a long and complex healing ceremony. An important part of this ceremony is the creation of sandpaintings.

This modern Navajo shaman is creating a sandpainting for a healing ceremony.

The singer is the Navajo **shaman**. He or she uses coloured sand to create a **sacred** design on a large piece of **buckskin**. The singer draws the spirits of animals and draws plants, such as corn, beans, squash and tobacco that have special healing powers. The painting's colours of white, blue, yellow and black symbolize dawn, daylight, twilight and night.

First, the sick person is purified with sweat baths. This means that he or she is placed in a small covered place where a fire is burning under a pot of water to create steam. The steam makes the person sweat all the bad things out of his or her body. After this, he or she kneels in the middle of the painting, facing east, and prays, often for days at a time, while the singer chants. When the healing ritual is over, the painting is swept away. The healing ceremony and sandpainting are ancient traditions. They have been important ceremonies in the Navajo culture for hundreds of years.

Sandpainting of a Yei God, Navajo shaman, western New Mexico, coloured sand, about 1985–1995CE.

Yei gods, like the one in this painting, are summoned by shamans to cure a sick person by pushing the bad spirits out of his or her body.

Bear sickness
The Navajo believe that nervousness, feeling faint and a troubled memory are all symptoms of a condition called bear sickness. This sickness can be caused by eating bear meat, killing a bear or dreaming about a bear. To cure bear sickness, the shaman makes a sandpainting and performs a ceremony called the Mountain Chant, or Mountaintop Way.

EARTH MOUNDS

Some of the most impressive Native American creations **archaeologists** have discovered are the more than 100,000 **earth mounds** found throughout the Eastern Woodlands **culture area** and in the Ohio and Mississippi River valleys. Many are small, simple mounds, but others are monumental works of art, built in the shape of birds or animals. Some are as large as the Great Pyramids of Egypt and can only be fully appreciated when they are viewed from the air. The Great Serpent Mound in Ohio is 410 m long, 6 m wide and 80 cm high.

Great Serpent Mound, Adena people, sculpted mound of earth and rock, near Locust Grove, Ohio, about 100BCE – 700CE.

*Some people think that the serpent mound was designed as a **ceremonial** calendar.*

The mounds were probably built over a period of several thousand years, from about 700BCE to about 1500CE by three main farming cultures: the Adena, the Hopewell and the Mississippian (also called the Natchez). Most were built as burial monuments and had a central chamber that contained the remains of important tribal members. Others were cemeteries for less important people, often containing 50 or more separately buried bodies. New mounds were often built on top of older ones from previous generations.

Objects that were buried with the dead, including pottery, **effigy pipes** and tools, were often made from materials such as copper, seashells and certain kinds of stone that were not readily available in the Eastern Woodlands. This tells archaeologists that the mound-building cultures must have traded over great distances with people from other culture areas.

Panorama of the Monumental Grandeur of the Mississippi Valley, *John J. Egan, about 1850CE.*

This painting shows archaeologists studying an earth mound in the Mississippi River valley.

NATIVE AMERICAN PAINTING

For thousands of years, Native American artists painted rocks, pottery and leather objects with images that reflected their **spiritual** beliefs, community history and pride. In the 19th and early 20th centuries, Native Americans were forced to give up their culture so they could blend into white America, and many Native American art forms disappeared. By the 1950s, institutions such as the Institute of American Indian Art began to encourage Native American artists to relearn their traditional art forms. Today, the nation's most important artists include Native Americans like Juane Quick-to-See Smith. These modern artists use traditional and **sacred** art forms to express new ideas.

Herd, *Juane Quick-to-See Smith,*
1998

In this painting, Smith has drawn outlines of a traditional image, the buffalo, over a collage made of articles and pictures that illustrate the mistreatment of Native Americans.

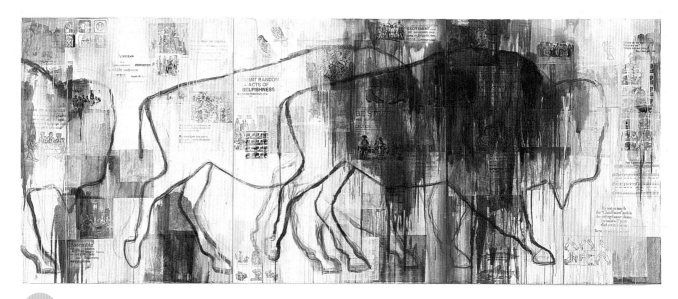

Make a buckskin painting

You will need:

strong brown wrapping paper, cut to make a large rectangle

crayons in colours such as brown, orange, red, black and yellow

newspapers

an iron

black permanent marker

white wax candle

1 Use the crayons to draw an image on the brown paper. Use the painting on page 5 for guidance. When your drawing is complete, rub the candle over all the areas of the paper that are not covered in crayon.

2 Crumple your picture into a ball, then open the paper up again. Repeat this about twenty times to make your picture look old and wrinkled. You can even step on the ball to make the wrinkles deeper.

3 Put your open picture between two layers of newspaper. Ask an adult to help you iron the newspaper that covers the top of your picture, until the wax begins to melt through the newspaper. Put an old towel on top of the newspaperr to protect the iron.

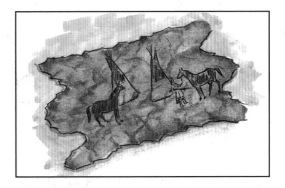

4 Remove your picture from the newspaper and go over the picture outlines in black permanent marker. Cut the picture into the shape of an animal hide. Your picture should have the wrinkled look and soft feel of a real buckskin painting.

TIMELINE

GLOSSARY

amulet ornament carried to protect the wearer

ancestor person from the past to whom someone is related to, such as a grandparent

animate give life to

archaeologist person who studies the past using objects made by people in the past

buckskin tanned deer hide used to make clothing, tents and other objects

ceremonial used in a ritual

clan group of people with something in common, who usually live together

cougar large wild cat found in North America. Also known as a puma.

culture areas region of the USA where there were several Native American groups that shared beliefs and customs

earth mounds massive burial sites that were often built in animal shapes

effigy pipe pipe carved to resemble a person or animal spirit

functional made to use in everyday living, or as part of religious ceremonies

gourd dried skin of fruits similar to pumpkins that are used as containers

limestone soft stone that is easy to carve

nomadic tending to move from place to place

petroglyphs pictures carved into rock to tell a story

pictograph painting on rock

pipestone soft, red stone, also called catlinite, that was used to make pipes

potlatch elaborate feast common in the Northwest Pacific Coast area, during which guests were given beautiful gifts

primitive simple, undeveloped

rattle musical instrument that makes a noise when it is shaken

ritual set of actions often performed as part of a religious ceremony

sacred highly respected, or worshipped

sacrifice losing or giving away something important for the good of others

serape woven cape worn over the shoulder

shaman Native American religious leader who can communicate with the spirits

spiritual having to do with religion

totem animal spirit used as a family symbol and for personal protection

trinket small object

unravel undo

vision quest spiritual journey made by young Native Americans to mark the change from child to adult

wampum beads made of shells or other valuable materials that were worn and also used as money

wigwam round shelter made of poles covered with bark or hides

INDEX